# Seasons Around You

# Spring

## Saviour Pirotta

**WAYLAND**

# Seasons Around You

 Autumn

 Spring

Summer

Winter

**Cover photograph:** Flying a kite in the spring.

**Title page:** A girl feeding milk to an orphan lamb.

Produced for Wayland Publishers Ltd by
Roger Coote Publishing
Gissing's Farm, Fressingfield
Eye, Suffolk IP21 5SH, England

Series designer: Jan Stirling
Book designer: Victoria Webb

First published in 1998 by
Wayland Publishers Limited
61 Western Road, Hove
East Sussex BN3 1JD, England

Find Wayland on the Internet at http://www.wayland.co.uk

**British Library Cataloguing in Publication Data**
Pirotta, Saviour, 1958–
    Spring. – (Seasons around you)
    1.Spring – Pictorial works – Juvenile literature
    I. Title
    508.2

ISBN 0 7502 2275 1

Printed and bound in Italy by EuroGrafica, Vicenza.

**Picture acknowledgements**
Angela Hampton Family Life Pictures 8, 23; Bubbles 1,
19 (Ian West); Chapel Studios 24 (Zul Mukhida), 25 (Zul
Mukhida); Eye Ubiquitous 29 (Bennett Dean); Frank Lane
Picture Agency 10 (E Poupinet/Sunset), 11 (François
Merlet), 12 (M J Thomas), 14 top (Simon Hosking), 14
bottom (W Howes), 15 top (M Rose), 15 bottom
(STF/Sunset), 16 (François Merlet), 17 (Martin Withers),
20 (E&D Hosking), 22 (E&D Hosking); Getty Images 6, 7
(David Hanover), 13 (Art Wolfe), 18 (Rosemary Calvert),
21 (Richard H Smith), 27 (Jerome Tisne), 28 (Leland
Bobbe); Image Bank 5 (Bokelberg); The Photographers
Library *front cover*; Tim Woodcock Photography 4, 9, 26.

# Contents

Words that appear in **bold** are explained in the glossary on page 32.

# Hello spring

What do you notice in spring?
The air gets warmer and the
days get longer.

We put away our thick winter clothes.
Lighter ones will do for a while.
We may still need our raincoats!

# Fun and games

Now the weather is warmer, it is fun to ride our bikes.

We can go out to play in the playground.
Sometimes we don't even need
to take our coats with us.

# Spring flowers

It's nice to go out for a walk in the park. The park is full of spring flowers – tulips, daffodils and bluebells.

Spring is a busy time for gardeners.
They plant poppies, **snapdragons** and
other flowers that will bloom in summer.

# Trees and leaves

Cherry and apple trees **blossom** all through April and May.

Out in the woods, bushes turn green.
Some trees grow soft clusters of tiny
flowers, called catkins.

# Animals in spring

Hedgehogs wake up from their winter sleep. They hunt around for food, enjoying the warmer air.

Animals and birds are finding **mates**.
They will have babies in spring or summer,
when there is plenty of food for them.

# Tadpoles and frogs

There is **frogspawn** in the fish tank at school. Some of the eggs are hatching into tadpoles.

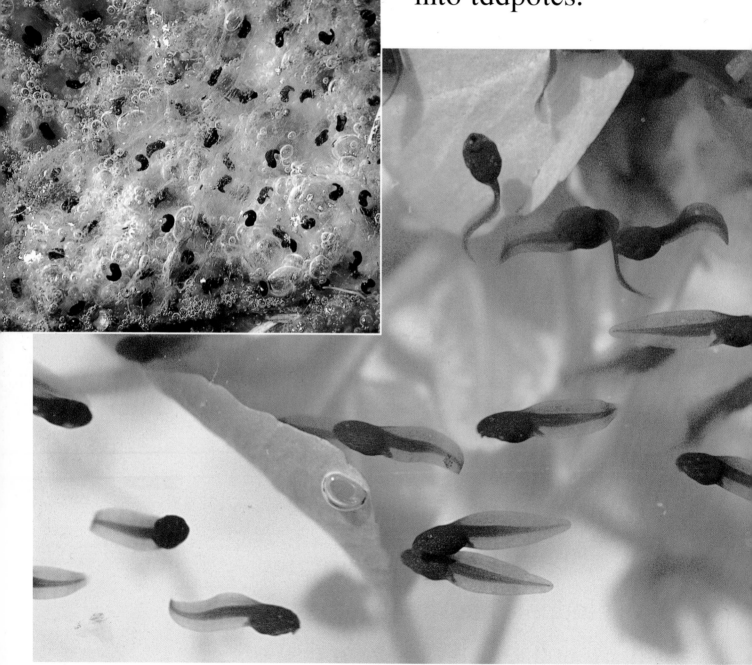

When the tadpoles have turned into baby
frogs, the teacher will put them in a pond.

# Here come the birds

Swallows return to the countryside from the south. Sparrows, starlings and other birds build their nests.

The blackbird has her chicks.
She feeds them worms and snails.
Then she flies away to find more food.

# Spring on the farm

There is lots to do on the farm.
Young lambs, calves, piglets and
foals are being born.

Sometimes baby lambs are **abandoned** by their mothers. They are orphan lambs. Orphan lambs have to be fed milk from a bottle.

# Growing crops

The farmers sow wheat and barley.
They will be ready to harvest in autumn.

Soon it is time to start harvesting
spring crops – cabbages, carrots,
broccoli and the first lettuces.

# Spring food

Gardeners get ready to pick their spring vegetables.

In spring we have light meals, like pasta and salads. It's nice to eat new potatoes and other spring vegetables.

# Pancake Day

On **Shrove Tuesday** we make pancakes.
We mix flour, milk and egg to make batter.
Then we cook the batter in a frying pan.

When one side of each pancake is cooked, we turn them over or ask an adult to toss them. Then we sprinkle them with sugar and lemon juice, roll them up and eat them.

# Easter

In spring we celebrate **Easter**.
At school we paint eggs and
make Easter cards.

We give each other chocolate Easter
eggs. Sometimes we hide them outside
and have an Easter egg hunt to find them.

# More spring festivals

Jewish families celebrate **Passover** in the spring. They have a special meal, called Seder, when they eat certain foods.

In the Hindu festival of **Holi**, people throw coloured powder at each other. They celebrate the arrival of colourful spring.

# Spring activities

 **GEOGRAPHY**

**Comparing localities** Find some pictures of the polar regions, a rain forest and a desert. How would spring there be different from spring where you live. Are there as many new plants growing? Are any animals waking up from hibernation?

 **DANCE AND DRAMA**

The festival of Holi celebrates the triumph of good over evil. Read the story of Holi, then make a dance about it. Holi is also the festival of colour, so don't forget to make your costumes as colourful as possible.

Create a play, charting the journey of a swallow from Egypt to the UK. You could include the sights and sounds the bird sees and hears as it crosses land and sea. What countries do you think it passes through?

**RE**

Celebrate Shrove Tuesday by making some pancakes. You could do this in class or at home with your family. You could even have a pancake party. Make lots of savoury fillings as well as sweet ones for the pancakes.

Find out what dishes are served for the special Seder meal at Passover. You could buy some of the foods at the shops and share them with your friends. Ask a teacher or a relative to tell you the story of Passover.

People in northern India celebrate Holi by drawing flower designs on the ground by their front door. Why don't you do the same by your classroom door? You could paint the patterns on white paper and tape the paper to the ground. Then you could invite your friends in and give them some sweets or cakes.

 **SCIENCE**

**See how they grow (systematic enquiry)** Make a collection of green leaves as they appear on bushes and trees. Label them carefully. Collect more leaves from the same trees every week. Can you measure how fast some leaves grow?

**Green plants as organisms** Carefully pull up a flowering weed from your garden or from the wildlife area in your school. Don't forget to ask an adult for permission first. Using books from your library, can you name the various parts of the plant?

**Variation and classification** Organize a nature watch. Sit with your friends very quietly in the garden and make a list of the living creatures you see. Can you find a name for them all? Can you divide the names on your list into birds, insects, animals and fish?

 **ART**

Decorate some hard-boiled eggs with Easter patterns. Then use the eggs to make mobiles for your room or class. Or you could give them to your friends as Easter gifts. You might even want to use them for an egg hunt at home or at school.

Design and make pop-up Easter cards. Decorate them with Easter symbols, like eggs, chicks, rabbits and lambs. Give or send the cards to your friends and family.

 **DESIGN AND TECHNOLOGY**

Some classes get very hot in spring. Design a shade to keep your class cool when the sun is blazing away. Keep all your notes, models and drawings and make an exhibition with them for the rest of the school to see.

# Topic web

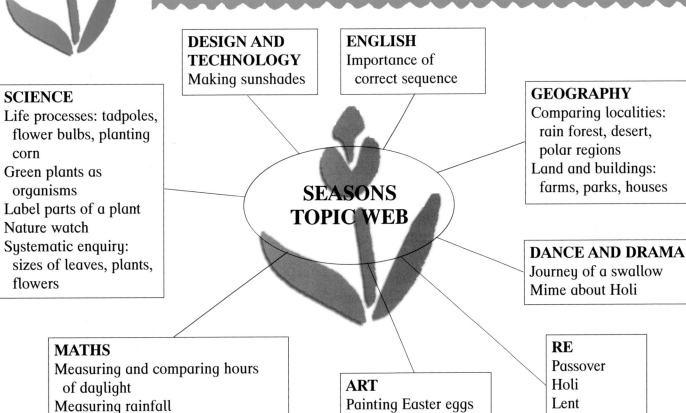

**DESIGN AND TECHNOLOGY**
Making sunshades

**ENGLISH**
Importance of
correct sequence

**SCIENCE**
Life processes: tadpoles,
  flower bulbs, planting
  corn
Green plants as
  organisms
Label parts of a plant
Nature watch
Systematic enquiry:
  sizes of leaves, plants,
  flowers

**GEOGRAPHY**
Comparing localities:
  rain forest, desert,
  polar regions
Land and buildings:
  farms, parks, houses

**SEASONS TOPIC WEB**

**DANCE AND DRAMA**
Journey of a swallow
Mime about Holi

**MATHS**
Measuring and comparing hours
  of daylight
Measuring rainfall
Sequence of seasons

**ART**
Painting Easter eggs
Making Easter cards

**RE**
Passover
Holi
Lent
Pancake Day

# Resources

**NON-FICTION**
*Weather Facts* by P. Eden and C. Twist
(Dorling Kindersley, 1995)

*The Seasons* by Debbie MacKinnon and Anthea
Sieveking (Frances Lincoln, 1997)

*From Snowflakes to Sandcastles* by Annie Owen
(Frances Lincoln, 1997)

*Passover* by Angela Wood (Wayland, 1997)

*A Seed in Need* by Sam Godwin (Macdonald
Young Books, 1998)

*Spring on the Farm* by Janet Fitzgerald (Evans, 1995)

*The World of Festivals* by Philip Steele (Macdonald
Young Books, 1996)

*Get Set, Go... Spring* by Ruth Thomson (Franklin
Watts, 1997)

**FICTION AND POETRY**
*Spring Story* by Jill Barklem (Collins Brambly
Hedge series, 1980). The adventures of the mice of
Brambly Hedge, with illustrations showing the
countryside in spring.

*Poems for Spring* by Robert Hull (Wayland, 1995).
Seasonal poems from around the world, illustrated
with colour photographs.

# Glossary

**Abandoned** Left behind. Animals such as sheep sometimes abandon one of the lambs they have just given birth to.

**Blossom** When a plant produces flowers.

**Easter** The day Jesus rose from the dead. It is one of the main festivals in the Christian calendar and it always falls on a Sunday.

**Frogspawn** Eggs laid by frogs.

**Holi** A Hindu festival celebrating the arrival of spring.

**Mates** Partners that will have young.

**Passover** A celebration when Jews remember how the Angel of Death spared their children in Egypt. It lasts eight days.

**Shrove Tuesday** The day before Lent begins. Also known as Pancake Day. In some countries people have a carnival.

**Snapdragons** Brightly coloured flowers that look like dragons' heads.

# Index